SONGS FROM A YAHI BOW

A SERIES OF POEMS ON ISHI

SONGS FROM A YAHI BOW

A SERIES OF POEMS ON ISHI

SCOTT EZELL

YUSEF KOMUNYAKAA

MIKE O'CONNOR

EDITED BY SCOTT EZELL

WITH AN ESSAY BY THOMAS MERTON

AND PAINTINGS BY JEFF HENGST

PLEASURE BOAT STUDIO
NEW YORK CITY

ISBN: 978-1-929355-67-9
Library of Congress Control Number: 2010942229

Design by Jason Schneiderman.

Pleasure Boat Studio books are available through the following:
SPD (Small Press Distribution) Tel. 800-869-7553, Fax 510-524-0852
Partners/West Tel. 425-227-8486, Fax 425-204-2448
Baker & Taylor 800-775-1100, Fax 800-775-7480
Ingram Tel 615-793-5000, Fax 615-287-5429
Amazon.com and bn.com

PLEASURE BOAT STUDIO: A LITERARY PRESS
www.pleasureboatstudio.com
201 West 89th Street
New York, NY 10024
Contact Jack Estes, Publisher
Fax: 888-810-5308

Email: pleasboat@nyc.rr.com

By placing one end of his bow at the corner of his open mouth and tapping the string with an arrow, the Yana could make sweet music. It sounded like an Aeolian harp. To this accompaniment Ishi sang a folksong telling of a great warrior whose bow was so strong that, dipping his arrow first in fire, then in the ocean, he shot at the sun. As swift as the wind, his arrow flew straight in the round open door of the sun and put out its light. Darkness fell upon the earth and men shivered with cold. To prevent themselves from freezing they grew feathers, and thus our brothers, the birds, were born.

—Saxton Pope, *Hunting with the Bow and Arrow*

TABLE OF CONTENTS

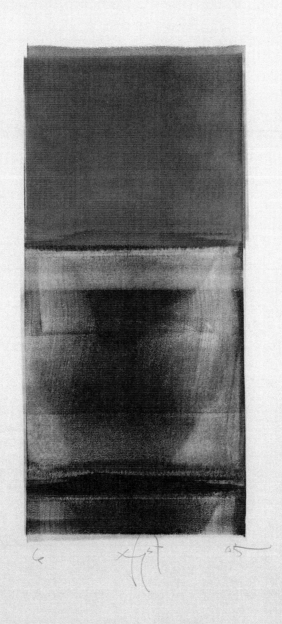

PREFACE:
FLASHES OF ISHI IN SUN-LIT STREAMS

> Ishi compels the imagination because with such un-
> assuming ease he affirms the supreme importance of
> ordinary human life.
>
> —Karl Kroeber

WITHIN THE INCREASING SPEED and complexity of society, one of the great challenges of contemporary life may be to retain a sense of wholeness in a world tending towards fragmentation. In late 2004, when I returned to California after living a dozen years in Asia, the last three of these in an aboriginal village on the Pacific coast of Taiwan, I felt pulled a hundred directions by the economic, ecological, political, and humanitarian crises that confronted me in my native land. Unpacking a box of books, I came across Theodora Kroeber's biography, *Ishi in Two Worlds*, and re-read this portrayal of a man in much more fractured conditions than my own, apparently facing his situation with day-to-day grace, humility, and good humor. At the time, I felt I was living in two worlds myself—between Asia and America; or, between a receding past and an inchoate future—without being home in either. Ishi, a Yahi Indian called for many decades "the last wild American Indian," moved from hunting and gathering to a modern industrial existence when in 1911 he emerged alone, the last of his tribe, from the westward drainages of Mount Lassen, in northern California, and lived the remaining five years of his life in San Francisco. Ishi seems to have remained whole, or "home" in both his original and adopted worlds, despite the trauma of this transition and the fact of his residence within the society that had extinguished his family, tribe, culture, and language.

I wrote my poem-cycle "Ishi" in the summer of 2005 as a re-imagining of Ishi in contemporary terms.[1] At that time, I lived in a dusty, low-income district of San Diego, and the landscape of my poems is an amalgamation

---

1. In writing "Ishi" I used a series of paintings by Jeff Hengst as sigils or windows through which to focus and reflect my thoughts on Ishi and my own experience.

of my daily environment with those of Ishi's life—both the chaparral hills where he was born and the San Francisco streets around the University of California Anthropology Museum, which became his home. "Ishi" was both an effort to express my own sense of living "in two worlds," and to conceive of the ability to "die at home wherever you may be."

That fall, I mentioned "Ishi" to poet Tim McNulty, as he kindly gave me a lift from Sequim, Washington, to a trailhead in the Olympic Mountains. Tim told me about a poem-cycle on Ishi which Mike O'Connor had written in the 1970s. We agreed it would be interesting to see the two works side by side, but it was not until two years later that I met Mike and had the chance to read his "Song of Ishi." The different perspectives and emphases of our Ishi poems, as well as the thirty year distance between them, created intriguing dynamics, and made us hope to publish them together as a book.

However, there was no obvious format or publisher for an Ishi book of contrasting poem-cycles. The idea lay fallow until February 2008, when I read Yusef Komunyakaa's "Quatrains for Ishi" in his *Thieves of Paradise*. At that point I began taking the idea of a book collection more seriously—I felt that these three works aggregated into a single, unified poetic sequence on Ishi, that was enriched by the dynamics between pieces written in different decades by poets of divergent backgrounds.[2] In addition, I thought that, taken together, these poems might reflect the evolution of a cultural relationship to Ishi as an archetype. Perhaps in the 1970s, Ishi existed in public consciousness as "what we have destroyed;" and by the 21st century maybe we have begun to recognize him as "what we are"—and to realize that as industrial society paves over ecosystems, languages, and indigenous cultures, we destroy not some abstraction or "other," but ourselves, and that the erosion of human and natural diversity diminishes us all.

I've appended Thomas Merton's 1968 essay "Ishi: A Meditation" to this poem-sequence to provide background information for readers not acquainted with Ishi, and because it serves as a chronological link between Theodora Kroeber's biography (1961) and Mike O'Connor's

---

2. This idea of a poetic construct in which the parts combine into an integrated whole has been the guiding principle of this book—it has never been conceived as an anthology. For this reason I have not included Ishi poems by well-known poets such as William Stafford and Louis Simpson.

"Song of Ishi," the first cycle of this collection. Merton's historical and spiritual perspective also places Ishi and his tribe in a larger cultural context, and I believe the connections Merton makes between the ethnocide of American Indians and the extermination mentality of the American-Vietnam war are still relevant today.

> No one has had more bleakly to confront, in total isolation, the destruction of everything that makes life worth living.
>
> —Karl Kroeber

A HUNDRED YEARS AGO, Ishi's individual experience anticipated many of the vast, global crises that have become manifest today: loss of habitat, extinction of languages and cultures, forced migration, genocide, and cultural assimilation. Still, in the midst of this devastation, and within "increasingly complex and hierarchical American culture,"[3] all I've read suggests that Ishi maintained a sense of individual and cultural identity, and related to others with friendliness and respect.[4] Ishi "busied himself almost from his first day at the museum, with adding to its collections [of] spears, and bows and arrows,"[5] a contiguity of craft which seemed to give him satisfaction and enjoyment, and perhaps helped sustain a connection to his original way of being. He visited the women's ward of the hospital next to the museum, holding patients' hands and offering wordless sympathy. He befriended children, one of whom reminisced half a century after Ishi's death that "No matter what he was doing he

---

3. Rachel Adams, "Ishi's Body: Anthropology and Popular Culture," *Ishi in Three Centuries*, p. 32.

4. Nancy Scheper-Hughes makes the important point that "there is a strong investment in believing that Ishi was a happy man who enjoyed his new life among his white friends, who was charmed by matches and window shades and was content in his new roles of janitor and living museum exhibit." She suggests he "was simply at the end of his existential rope," but adds that Ishi "accepted his final destiny with patience, good humor, and grace." Nancy Scheper-Hughes, "Ishi's Brain, Ishi's Ashes: Anthropology and Genocide," *Ishi in Three Centuries*, p. 119.

5. Theodora Kroeber, *Ishi in Two Worlds*, p. 184

would glance up from time to time and smile…To me, he will never be gone completely as long as I can remember his great kindness, patience, and understanding towards me."[6]

As contemporary society and individual choices become increasingly polarized, personal dignity seems more and more difficult to cultivate. We are living within a pandemic of solastalgia—homesickness when one has not left home.[7] The world as we know it, the things that make our earth house "home," are disappearing. The forms of destruction Ishi faced in isolation are now part of everyday consciousness on a mass scale, both through direct experience and through media cycles that are often little more than headline compendiums of tragedy. In this context of mounting catastrophe, I think many of us would aspire to Karl Kroeber's assertion about Ishi's ability to live without self-pity or a sense of victimhood: "I do not see how we can speak of his life as anything but tragic, yet I have come to feel that he himself did not so regard it."[8]

Practically from the moment he emerged from the wilderness into White America, Ishi has been turned into a symbol of something lost—labeled the last wild Indian, the last uncontaminated Indian, the last Yahi, etc. He certainly was the last of something, but of exactly what we will never know. Ishi's history, personality, and experience can't be fit into a tidy label, and it's necessary to qualify almost any description we apply to him. Though he was the last Native American in the continental United States to live by traditional hunting and gathering, or "tending the wild" (M. Kat Anderson's phrase), he incorporated foraged "non-native" materials into his handicraft, such as discarded bottle glass to carve arrowheads, and iron nails for harpoon points. Moreover, his upbringing was anything but typical of what the phrase "wild Indian" evokes—by the time Ishi was born, most of California's native cultures had been

---

6. Fred H. Zumwalt Jr., "A Personal Remembrance of Ishi," *Ishi in Three Centuries*, p. 17.

7. "Solastalgia," a term coined by Glenn Albrecht, refers to the loss of "physical and sensory signals that define home," such as the disappearance of familiar birds and plants as climates change, which leads to a sense of displacement similar to those felt by "indigenous populations that are forcibly removed from their traditional homelands," though one has not left home. Clive Thompson, "The Next Victim of Climate Change? Our Minds." *Wired* Magazine, January 2008.

8. Karl Kroeber, "The Humanity of Ishi," *Ishi in Three Centuries*, p. 143.

ruptured or displaced by the Gold Rush, with its massive incursion of white settlers seizing land, and by the "Indian Wars" and vigilante attacks that resulted from conflicts between Whites and Indians. Clan and tribe dynamics, which had shaped and defined American Indian communities for centuries, had been disrupted or discarded in the decades of war and concealment during which Ishi was born and lived in the wilderness. There's irony in the conception of Ishi as the "last wild Indian,"[9] in that his tribal existence was not pure and free, as the term "wild" suggests in it's romanticized usage, but rather determined by war, intense social and material stress, isolation, divestment, and the impossibility of reproducing. Though he acquired the technical, natural, and hunting knowledge and skills of his tribe, and could sing dozens of Yahi songs from memory, Ishi was born into a contorted social structure and the specter of extinction.

Ishi was almost certainly the last Yahi speaker (a sub-group of the Yana tribe and language), but recent scholarship has called into question many long-standing assumptions about his background. Studies of Ishi's facial structure and arrow point shapes suggest he was in part ethnically and culturally Wintu or Nomlaki, tribes that neighbored the Yana: "What emerges from these historical details and archaeological inference is a picture of an amalgam culture by the early to mid-nineteenth century where a Wintu/Nomlaki-Yahi boy learned to produce projectile points as a Wintu/Nomlaki but lived the life of a Yahi in the Lassen foothills until no more Yahi remained."[10]

Most of the facts of Ishi's life will remain forever unknown, including his true name—he never broke his tribe's taboo against speaking one's own name. "Ishi," an Anglicization of *I'citi*, the Yahi word for "man," was chosen as an appellation by anthropologist Alfred Kroeber. (In fact, he observed this prohibition to the degree that once "Ishi" became his name, he was never heard to speak that word again.) His patrimony, the nature of his upbringing, and details of his 40 years in hiding will never be known, in part because he demurred from speaking of the dead.[11] Larger

---

9. Concow Maidu artist Frank Tuttle expresses this irony in his Ishi painting, "What Wild Indian?"

10. "The Stone Tool Technology of Ishi and the Yana," by M. Steven Shackley, *Ishi in Three Centuries*, p. 193.

11. Almost all the Yahi had been killed by 1870. Ishi survived in the foothills of

cultural or demographic enigmas also abide, subterranean, beneath what we see and know of Ishi. For example, the Yana arrow-release technique Ishi used "was unlike that of any other people in the New World, but was identical with the release of ancient China."[12] This fact suggests deep roots and vast, complex migrations that will probably never be traced or understood, except in terms of mystery and wonder.

"Ishi lent a face, a name, and a personalized narrative to the genocide of his people…Ishi came to represent more than the life of a single man and to symbolize instead, the broader experience of Native Americans."[13] Considering the strands of history, culture, and personality that converged in him, it's inevitable that Ishi has become a symbol. However, Ishi's manifold and sophisticated individuality has sometimes been flattened or obscured, or appropriated to fit a pre-molded history or mythology. Yusef Komunyakaa suggests the danger of this in "Quatrains for Ishi," when he writes, "I know if I see you / as me, you'll disappear." To compress Ishi into an icon detracts from the larger dimensions of personal courage and dignity he demonstrated in facing the vulnerability and uncertainty of his life. Such oversimplification is a form of self-impoverishment in an age when we lack such concrete affirmations of human experience.

Ishi's life "demanded the capacity to improvise, adapt, and endure at every step along the way,"[14] which in our changing world is increasingly required, to different degrees, of almost everyone. I personally relate to Ishi as a reminder of something or many things that are irretrievably past, but also as an example of regeneration, and the integrity and suppleness of spirit that may come with being "home" in one's own skin. At its best, poetry has the potential to explore the seam between the known and unknown, between concrete facts and mystery, and to express complexities, contradictions, and subtleties without reducing them to moral or cultural imperatives. Corresponding with the 100th anniversary of his emergence, I hope *Songs from a Yahi Bow* presents Ishi

---

Mt. Lassen with a small band of a dozen that gradually diminished until he was the sole survivor when he emerged in 1911.

12. Robert F. Heizer and Theodora Kroeber, eds., *Ishi the Last Yahi: A Documentary History*, p. 2.

13. Nancy Scheper-Hughes, "Ishi's Brain, Ishi's Ashes: Anthropology and Genocide." *Ishi in Three Centuries*, p. 118

14. Orin Starn, *Ishi's Brain*, p. 246.

not just as the last of something, but also as an enduring possibility for new beginning—an expansive and resonant human being, irreducible, standing taller than the circumstances of his life seemed to allow:

> Even now I can picture
> the salmon flashing
> in the sun-lit streams
> and the tender clover
> bursting through the rock.[15]

Scott Ezell
Hanoi
Summer 2010

---

15. From "Late Winter Dream Song," Mike O'Connor, "Song of Ishi."

SONG OF ISHI

MIKE O'CONNOR

When Blue Jay Goes to Bed

Smoke from a tended fire
curls above a brush shelter
in the madrone trees.

A woman with baby and basket
calls to the man fishing
waist-deep in the Yuna River.

Grandmother looks up
from her bead work;

Elder looks up
from his arrow-making.

The last light is rose on the volcano—
and now falls the wing of a crow.

Words of a Yahi Tribesman

I hate to leave this river
and the hills my people love.
Who are these strangers
who bring us sickness, war and death?

Spirit, my people have listened
to your presence:
> in the laughter of salmon's river,
> in the rustling leaves of crow's pine.

You know the joy
> the acorn's ripeness brings,
> the delight the tiny huckleberry holds.

Oak, scrub pine and lush meadows . . .
I am dizzy with ignorance.
You know what I can't know,
> see what I can't see;

but even though the stars over the western ocean
> should one
> by one
>> go out . . .

Rapid as We Vanish

My digging stick I break
and take up the hunting bow.
Yesterday at the caves,
six of our people gunned down in surprise.
Whiteman is more driven
than the spawning salmon.
What evil comes upon this land
swifter than a cloud covering the moon?

Now we place a rock cairn to mark
our people's place. Now,
and everywhere,
    the cropped heads of our mourning women
        —like uncovered wild bulbs—
           rapid as we vanish,

                appear.

Song of Ishi

To breast the swift river
on a hot clear day;
to rope-climb a towering
canyon wall;
stalk, gut and skin
the beautiful deer;
pound up acorn
into meal.

At feast time after harvest,
I am crazy with love.
In winter, I make a new bow.

Caught in a rainstorm,
buckskin keeps my fire drill dry.

Hare snare for small fishing;
double prong poon for the salmon.

Eagle, buzzard, blue jay
feather my arrows;
tail of a wildcat
to put them in.

Children, mush and lots of singing;
strike of a rattler; flick of a bowstring.

Waganupa foothill wilderness,
years ago.

Ishie Shantie

Sitshum skookum chuck
kopa hyas waum klah sun;
lope klatawa sagalie hyas tall
tanino skookum kullah;
mamook hunt, mamook gut pe mamook skin
kloshe mowitch;
kokshut tukwilla
kopa sapolil.

Kopa hiyu muckamuck kimtah iskum sapolil
nika pelton kopa ticky.
Cole illahee nika mamook chee opitlkegh.

Kopa hiyu snass
man mowitch skin kloshe nanitch nika piah stick.

Kwitshadie lepiege kopa tenas pish;
lapushet kopa sammon.

Chakchak, buzzard, spooh kalakala
tupso nika kalitan;
opoots hyas pusspuss
mahsh klaska kopa.

Hiyu tenas, mush pe hiyu shantie;
shugh opoots pight elip; opitlkegh tenas lope latlah.

Waganupa lepee tenas saghalie illahee lemolo illahee
ahnkuttie.

Late Winter Dream Song

Over the smoke hole
rides the last snow moon.
A spring wind retrieves the rain.

Even now I can picture
the salmon flashing
in the sun-lit streams
and the tender clover
bursting through the rock.

Arrow whizzing from a new drawn bow:
        fresh deer meat!
I will dance and sing for six days!

Summer

Sleeping rattlesnake, it's too hot to strike.
Cool tastes the pounded manzanita.
We fish in the early morning hours,
swim in the afternoon.
Learn the stars in the open night sky,
go to Waganupa, to the shade
of her slopes and tall trees.

Hunting summer fat deer,
     hunting the breeze.

Rattle Song

Fawn cry, arrow whiz,
snake rattle, coyote yip,
water fall, timber creak,
fire crackle, wind pine roar.

Grizzly growl, dove moan,
insect buzz, raven call,
       stone flake click,
           fire drill whirr,
rain drip, squirrel squeak,

    bare foot steps.

Down from the Hills

Long ago I left off hiding.
Twelve of us were a nation;
five of us were a nation—
I alone am nothing left.

Old Coyote Doctor, you can't hurt me now.
The bones of my people are scattered like chaparral
    through the foothills.
Yuna Creek is as blank as a night of snow.
The last deer has gone to the volcano.
Little rabbit, I would rather starve than kill you.
Old Coyote Doctor, you can't hurt me now.
Loneliness was your best arrow:
sharper than hunger, more accurate than fear.
I'm tired now.
I have crossed the boundary of my people's land
and the boundary of Coyote Night.

In the east, beyond that stick corral,
where Whiteman's dogs
are barking an alarm,

          that rose in the heavens
          must be the dawn.

Ishi in Town

A plane is nothing when you see the Hawk.
Don't feel bad, but a skyscraper
        is a poor mountain.
    I like this penny whistle very much,
  but it won't call rabbits.
        Whiskey is amber as upper Mill Creek,
    but it's crazy fire.
I must hold my laughing sides
      when I see typewriter.
    Old Salmon leaps up rapids
     a boat can't float down,

     but all in all
      I like these pockets
       in my pants.

You Stay, I Go

"Everybody hoppy?"
March 25th, 1916,
the last wild Indian of America is dead.
Tubercle bacillus—
like an arrow to his lung.

"Everybody hoppy?"
Yahi-Medicine-Old-Man Kuwi,
keep Coyote Doctor from our door.

Like an arrow to his lung—
and smoke to the four directions
can't cure him,
can't suck out the pain.

"Do you believe in God?"
"Sure, Mike."

And his spirit flies the burning body
        to the Land of the Dead,
where the oak, scrub pine and lush meadows
        whisper his secret name,

        to the Land of the Dead,
where sidewalks, trolley cars and playgrounds
        whisper his secret name . . .

        Ishi having crossed all the Realms.

Thinking of Ishi While Reading the Want Ads

Hairstylist
Furnace Installer
Jobs! Jobs! Jobs!
Data Processor
Nickel Alloy Machinist
Daily Delivery, Monday thru Sunday
Are You an Elephant? Why Work for Peanuts?
Hunter/Gatherer
Activist Minded? Use Our Phone Bank.
Taxi Driver. Must Have Washington License.

Ishi and the Braves

He wouldn't have been insulted
by the war chants or the "chop":
he wouldn't have understood them!

Nation, tribe wiped out
when he'd only known how many springs;
and you don't throw a tomahawk
at salmon or deer.

But he would have been interested in,
and nervous of, the crowd,
just as he had been more curious
about the audience at the vaudeville show,
Berkeley, 1912, than about the show itself.

He knew people, but he didn't know groups.

The ball game under the great lights
of the stadium in Atlanta, Georgia
would have played on below him,
a sideshow of jugglers and clowns
as against the spectacle of 60 thousand
cheering, demonstrative Atlantans.

"More people than stars," he might have mused.

•

The multi-millionaire slugger
pulls a high fastball screaming
toward the left-field stands
right at Ishi,
and the hunter-gatherer of Yuna Creek,

surprised, shoots up his arm
and nails it on the fly.

The multitudinous Atlantans
seeing this directly,
or on the wide outfield monitor,
explode with happiness,
believing that this squat,
middle-aged Indian, now standing
before them, still holding the ball,
is the promotional genius of baseball
and not, in a million years,
the "last wild Indian" of America.

•

"Atlanta is ours and fairly won,"
General William Tecumseh Sherman,
in a wire to Abraham Lincoln,
September 2, 1862
two days before Sherman's army
burned Atlanta to the ground.

Notes

"Song of Ishi" is a poem cycle derived from Theodora Kroeber's book: *Ishi in Two Worlds*. Gary Snyder has referred to Ishi as ". . . surely the patron Bodhisattva of our Northern California nation . . ." Or, of any place, really, where civilization encroaches on wilderness.

"Ishi Shantie" is a Chinook Jargon rendering of the cycle's title poem, "Song of Ishi." The English and Chinook Jargon have a line-by-line correspondence.

Waganupa is the same mountain known today as Lassen in Northern California.

Special thanks to poet Don Jordan, Cheyenne Nation.

"Song of Ishi" is for Michael Daley.

QUATRAINS FOR ISHI

YUSEF KOMUNYAKAA

When they swoop on you hobbled there
almost naked, encircled by barking dogs
at daybreak beside a slaughterhouse
in Oroville, outside Paradise,

California, draped in a canvas scrap
matted with dung & grass seed,
slack-jawed men aim rifles
at your groin. *Wild Man*

hums through telegraph wires,
as women from miles around
try to tame your tongue
by cooking family recipes

& bringing bowls of ambrosia
to the jail. Hungry & sick,
lonely & scared, you never touch
the food. Not even the half-breeds

can open your mouth with Wintu,
Spanish, & Maidu. Days pass
till an anthropologist faces you
with his list of lost words,

rolling them off his tongue
like beads of old honey. But you
are elsewhere, covering your head
with a mourning cap of pine pitch,

in earshot of Wild Horse Corral,
as winds steal prayers of the dead
from Kingsley Cave. It takes
more than years of moonlight

to torch bones down to ashes
to store in a rock cairn
at Mill Creek. You are there,
Ishi, with the last five men

strong enough to bend bows,
with the last twelve voices
of your tribe. When you hear
the anthropologist say *siwini*,

the two of you dance
& bang your hands against
the wooden cot, running fingers
along the grain of yellow pine.

On Main Street, where gold
fever left the air years ago,
you're now The Wild Man of Oroville
beside a new friend. When the train

whistles, you step behind a cottonwood
shading the platform, afraid of The Demon
your mother forbade you to venture near.
What is it, does a voice call to you

out of windy chaparral,
out of Wowunupo mu tetna,
to urge you back? Down
that rainbow of metal light

& sparks—then ferried across
Carquinez Straits—to the Oakland Mole.
The Golden Gate frames water
meeting the sky, as a trolley car

lumbers uphill to your new home
at the Museum of Anthropology.
Here, in this ancient dust
on artifacts pillaged from Egypt

& Peru, I know why a man like you
laughs with one hand over his mouth.
Also, I know if I think of you
as me, you'll disappear. Ishi,

you're like a Don Juan
sitting beside Mrs. Gifford
calling birds. Who's Miss Fannie
in this photo from St. Louis?

Friend, what can you say
about these stone charms
from Lone Pine & England,
& are you still going to Chico

for that *Fiesta Arborea?*
How about this Sierra Club
walk from Buena Vista Park?
Here's another sack of acorns,

a few bundles of buckeye, hazel
shoots & alder. There's a sadness
in these willow branches, but no mock
orange. Pine needles have taught me

humility, & and I'll never string
a bow or chip a blade from a block
of obsidian. The salmon harpoon
glides through the air as if

your mind entered the toggles
& shaft. I walk backwards
into Bear's Hiding Place
like you showed me—coming when

gone, on the other side of the river
standing here beside you, a snare
of milkweed coiled on the ground
like a curse inside a dream.

Back in your world of leaves,
you journey ten thousand miles
in a circle, hunted for years
inside the heart, till you wake

talking to a shadow in a robe
of wildcat pelts. Here
the day's bright as the purse
you carry your sacred tobacco in.

Your lungs are like thumbprints
on a negative, with you at a hospital
window as workmen walk girders:
All a same monkey-tee. I know why

a man doesn't sleep with the moon
in his face, how butter steals
the singing voice, & how a frog
cures a snakebite. At the museum

in your counting room, we gaze
down at the divided garden, past
beaded phantoms on streetcorners
perfumed with incense & herbs,

signalling the hills closer
where eucalyptus stores up oils
for a new inferno in the Sutro
Forest. Here's your five hundred

& twenty half dollars
saved in thirteen film cases—
your unwound watch now ticks
as the pot of glue hardens

among your arrows & knots
of deer sinews. March 25
at noon is as good a time to die
as to be born. A bluish sun

conspires to ignite the pyre
of bone awls & pendants of Olivella
shells, as a bear stands in Deer Creek
waving a salmon at the sky.

—for Luzma

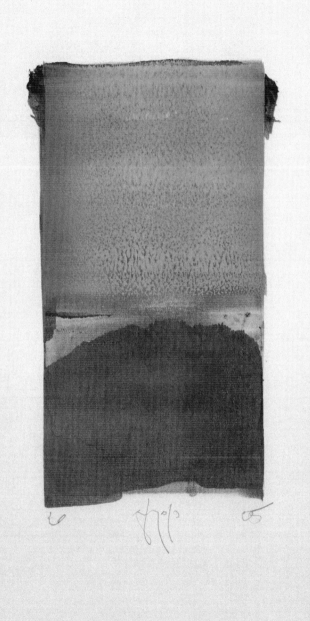

ISHI

SCOTT EZELL

> Die into what the earth requires of you.
> —Wendell Berry

1.

square tongues   speak brick words
   that couple into nothing,
   surrounded by hair and flowers.

decay of fruit and love and sex,
   all subside
         into chemical contemplation,
     alcohol and buzzing bees,
      sweet sticky scents.

         police machines   chop the sky
         into thistles of noise and fear—

I pick up and carry a river on my back,
a cloak of home
     to drape across
        the shoulders of the world,
         enfolding streams and stones.

glaze of bone
across my eyes,
a hood of silence,

my tongue of salt
dissolving into words
I speak to you.

2.

secrets of myself
I discover and discard a thousand times
    flower from your skin,
      seeds of me grown
        from the soil of you.

I am a benevolent bear,
wasted with circus tricks.

I am iron claws,
    and seize you with
      die-cast hands.
    we are chains and cages,
        we are free.

3.

I am an adze of bone,
and scrape at refinery
        dross and efflux,
      the slag of engine heat.

wild birds fly sky trails
        beyond my vision.
     reams of light stack page by page
       across the slush and bray
            of slaughterhouse corrals.

I am a scaffolding of planed horizons,
ghost mountains rise within my veins.

4.

I drop a cigarette in the gutter
      and flow
  crustacean to the sea.

scull the sky with matchsticks,
                scratch and flare
    but compend to nothing,
        pass a flame
          to a newspaper,
          to a forest fire,
              to a cock or cunt
            to singe the earth
              with zygote need—

      manzanita
    grows gold and gnarled
      from ash and char,

chikakatee, chikakatee,
quail gather and alight
in the cut lawns of city parks.

5.

I am a gravel truck of tar and meat,
petroglyphs of diesel brain.

flicker and glare
of tv memory,
    my tongue is obsidian
                arrow blades.

I am a butcher's apron
    laid between two mountains,
  a blue river flows
        from my stains and folds.

6.

white noise brainwaves
  bleed the sky,
robot sun
    stands from a crack of stone
        into a void of girder ribs,
            conduits pulse
                and circle through.

          I miss the mouth to the interior of you,
          the cleft of hair and skin
                where I recline with boneyard flowers,
                    half-drunk
                    half-happy
                    half-dead,
                        and drink soil soup,
                    broth of toenails and beards.

  —condom wrappers
  along the morning sidewalk,
  torn silver lining, pale
  lubricant sheen—

a million engines
crumple and rust
across my skin,
I am a
scrap metal wilderness,
a myth of one,
a heart spindle
coiled in wires of
    memory.

7.

monolith skies
   sift discount coupons
   across a blur of freeway speed, concrete furrows
      plowed by gasoline.

             pubic middens
             of pottery and teeth
             aggregate into engines.

  insurrection thoughts
          hang out on corners
           in baggy jeans
            and black bandanas,
           bailbond ads smile from the backs of
             bus stop benches,

                bottles break into blades,
                power lines dissect the sky.

8.

take a bucket of turpentine and
   a wire brush,
abrade
   the surface of the sky,
reveal
   reflections of yourself
like the scratched and dented tin
   of a subway station mirror,
like the aluminum glint
   between four fingers
holding two dozen nickels worth
   of brownbag beer.

      now
      I am the city,
     radio static within
         a bottle heart,
         ruled components of
         breath and stone.

rainbow oil, primer gray
   suburban streets,
susurrus of
   broken leaves—
peel electric skin
   from clouds and rain,
strip
   to bulbous core,
America, sink
   your longiphallic soul
into the sea,

let the world
begin
    again.

9.

I am ursine hibernation,
    dark and matted,
    I reek and sleep
    through storms of steel decay.

you are the further shore
    across a sea of metal brine,
    petrol flowers bloom
    from the burrow of your womb.

distance shellacs the wholeness of me,
currents of plankton flow between us.

10.

dust trails across a bath of sperm,
    I am abstraction   seized.

headlines slice the streets
open into purple flowers,
sirens unzip the sky and
        beneath the blue it wears a suit and tie.
 old bums with birdnest beards
           suck wine and nicotine
      by the back doors
         of strip tease matinees—

         a man in rubber gloves
          whistles a tune,
        sprays corrosion
          onto the green that grows
        from sidewalk cracks.

outside a bar,
an american flag is
stuck to a wall
with chewing gum—
by a silvered window
a polyester girl
worries a diamond ring,
mouth painted red,
hair bleached white,
eyes of plastic blue.

grease and alcohol
  brayered into
          approximations of self,
    the asphalt hush that
day after day I drive—

    photographic visions
    washed in a stop bath of departure,

        die at home wherever you may be.

ISHI: A MEDITATION

THOMAS MERTON

GENOCIDE IS A NEW WORD. Perhaps the word is new because technology has now got into the game of destroying whole races at once. The destruction of races is not new—just easier. Nor is it a specialty of totalitarian regimes. We have forgotten that a century ago white America was engaged in the destruction of entire tribes and ethnic groups of Indians. The trauma of California gold. And the vigilantes who, in spite of every plea from Washington for restraint and understanding, repeatedly took matters into their own hands and went out slaughtering Indians. Indiscriminate destruction of the "good" along with the "bad"—just so long as they were Indians. Parties of riffraff from the mining camps and saloons suddenly constituted themselves defenders of civilization. They armed and went out to spill blood and gather scalps. They not only combed the woods and canyons—they even went into the barns and ranch houses, to find and destroy the Indian servants and hired people, in spite of the protests of the ranchers who employed them.

The Yana Indians (including the Yahi or Mill Creeks) lived around the foothills of Mount Lassen, east of the Sacramento River. Their country came within a few miles of Vina where the Trappist monastery in California stands today. These hill tribes were less easy to subdue than their valley neighbors. More courageous and more aloof, they tried to keep clear of the white man altogether. They were not necessarily more ferocious than other Indians, but because they kept to themselves and had a legendary reputation as "fighters," they were more feared. They were understood to be completely "savage." As they were driven further and further back into the hills, and as their traditional hunting grounds gradually narrowed and emptied of game, they had to raid the ranches in order to keep alive. White reprisals were to be expected, and they were ruthless. The Indians defended themselves by guerilla warfare. The whites decided that there could be no peaceful coexistence with such neighbors. The Yahi, or Mill Creek Indians, as they were called, were marked for complete destruction. Hence they were regarded as sub-human. Against them there were no restrictions and no rules. No treaties need be made for no Indian could be trusted. Where was the point in "negotiation?"

Ishi, the last survivor of the Mill Creek Indians, whose story was published by the University of California at Berkeley in 1964[1], was born during the war of extermination against his people. The fact that the last Mill Creeks were able to go into hiding and to survive for another fifty years in their woods and canyons is extraordinary enough. But the courage, the resourcefulness, and the sheer nobility of these few stone age men struggling to preserve their life, their autonomy and their identity as a people rises to the level of tragic myth. Yet there is nothing mythical about it. The story is told with impeccable objectivity—though also with compassion—by the scholars who finally saved Ishi and learned from him his language, his culture, and his tribal history.

To read this story thoughtfully, to open one's heart to it, is to receive a most significant message: one that not only moves, but disturbs. You begin to feel the inner stirrings of that pity and dread which Aristotle said were the purifying effect of tragedy. "The history of Ishi and his people," says the author, Theodora Kroeber, "is inexorably part of our own history. We have absorbed their lands into our holdings. Just so must we be the responsible custodians of their tragedy, absorbing it into our tradition and morality." Unfortunately, we learned little or nothing about ourselves from the Indian wars.

"They have separated murder into two parts and fastened the worse on me"—words which William Carlos Williams put on the lips of a Viking Exile, Eric the Red. Men are always separating murder into two parts: one which is unholy and unclean: for "the enemy." Another which is a sacred duty: "for our side." He who first makes the separation, in order that he may kill, proves his bad faith. So too in the Indian wars. Why do we always assume the Indian was the aggressor? We were in *his* country, we were taking it over for ourselves, and we likewise refused even to share any with him. We were the people of God, always in the right, following a manifest destiny. The Indian could only be a devil. But once we allow ourselves to see all sides of the question, the familiar perspectives of American history undergo a change. The "savages" suddenly become human and the "whites," the "civilized," can seem barbarians. True, the

---

1. *Ishi In Two Worlds: A biography of the last wild Indian in North America*, by Theodora Kroeber. (University of California Press, Berkeley, 1964) [Merton may refer to a later edition of the book; it was originally published in 1961. —Ed.]

Indians were often cruel and inhuman (some more than others). True also, the humanity, the intelligence, the compassion and understanding which Ishi met with in his friends the scholars, when he came to join our civilization, restore the balance in our favor. But we are left with a deep sense of guilt and shame. The record is there. The Mill Creek Indians, who were once seen as bloodthirsty devils, were peaceful, innocent and deeply wronged human beings. In their use of violence they were, so it seems, generally very fair. It is we who were the wanton murderers, and they who were the innocent victims. The loving kindness lavished on Ishi in the end did nothing to change that fact. His race had been barbarously, pointlessly destroyed.

The impact of the story is all the greater because the events are so deeply charged with a natural symbolism: the structure of these happenings is such that it leaves a haunting imprint on the mind. Out of that imprint come disturbing and potent reflections.

Take for example the scene in 1870 when the Mill Creeks were down to their last twenty or thirty survivors. A group had been captured. A delegation from the tiny remnant of the tribe appeared at a ranch to negotiate. In a symbolic gesture, they handed over five bows (five being a sacred number) and stood waiting for an answer. The gesture was not properly understood, though it was evident that the Indians were trying to recover their captives and promising to abandon all hostilities. In effect, the message was: "Leave us alone, in peace, in our hills, and we will not bother you any more. We are few, you are many, why destroy us? We are no longer any menace to you." No formal answer was given. While the Indians were waiting for some intelligible response, one of the whites slung a rope over the branch of a tree. The Indians quietly withdrew into the woods.

From then on, for the next twelve years, the Yahi disappeared into the hills without a trace. There were perhaps twenty of them left, one of whom was Ishi, together with his mother and sister. In order to preserve their identity as a tribe, they had decided that there was no alternative but to keep completely away from white men, and have nothing whatever to do with them. Since co-existence was impossible, they would try to be as if they did not exist for the white man at all. To be there as if they were not there.

In fact, not a Yahi was seen. No campfire smoke rose over the trees.

Not a trace of fire was found. No village was discovered. No track of an Indian was observed. The Yahi remnant (and that phrase takes on haunting biblical resonances) systematically learned to live as invisible and as unknown.

To anyone who has ever felt in himself the stirrings of a monastic or solitary vocation, the notion is stirring. It has implications that are simply beyond speech. There is nothing one can say in the presence of such a happening and of its connotations for what our spiritual books so glibly call "the hidden life." The "hidden life" is surely not irrelevant to our modern world; nor is it a life of spiritual comfort and tranquility which a chosen minority can happily enjoy, at the price of a funny costume and a few prayers. The "hidden life" is the extremely difficult life that is forced upon a remnant that has to stay completely out of sight in order to escape destruction.

This so called "long concealment" of the Mill Creek Indians is not romanticized by any means. The account is sober, objective, though it cannot help being an admiring tribute to the extraordinary courage and ingenuity of these lost stone-age people. Let the book speak for itself.

> The long concealment failed in its objective to save a people's life but it would seem to have been brilliantly successful in its psychology and techniques of living...Ishi's group was a master of the difficult art of communal and peaceful coexistence in the presence of alarm and in a tragic and deteriorating prospect...
>
> It is a curious circumstance that some of the questions which arise about the concealment are those for which in a different context psychologists and neurologists are trying to find answers for the submarine and outer space services today. Some of these are: what makes for morale under confining and limiting life-conditions? What are the presumable limits of claustrophobic endurance?...It seems that the Yahi might have qualified for outer space had they lasted into this century.

There is something challenging and awe inspiring about this thoughtful passage by a scientifically trained mind. And that phrase about "qualifying for outer space" has an eerie ring about it. Does someone pick up the half-heard suggestion that the man who wants to live a normal life span during the next two hundred years of our history must be the kind of person who is "qualified for outer space?" Let us return to Ishi. The following sentences are significant:

> In contrast to the Forty-niners…whose mentality and morale had crumbled, Ishi and his band remained incorrupt, humane, compassionate, and with their faith intact even unto starvation, pain and death. The questions then are: what makes for stability? For psychic strength? For endurance, courage, faith?

The answers given by the author to these questions are mere suggestions. The Yahi were on their own home ground. This idea is not developed. The reader should reflect a little on the relation of the Indian to the land on which he lived. In this sense, most modern men never know what it means to have a "home ground." Then there is a casual reference to the "American Indian mystique" which could also be developed. William Faulkner's hunting stories, particularly "The Bear," give us some idea of what this "mystique" might involve. The word "mystique" has unfortunate connotations: it suggests an emotional icing on an ideological cake. Actually the Indian lived by a deeply religious wisdom which can be called in a broad sense mystical, and that is certainly much more than "a mystique." The book does not go into religious questions very deeply, but it shows us Ishi as a man sustained by a deep and unassailable spiritual strength which he never discussed.

Later, when he was living "in civilization," and was something of a celebrity as well as an object of charitable concern, Ishi was questioned about religion by a well-meaning lady. Ishi's English was liable to be unpredictable, and the language of his reply was not within its own ironic depths of absurdity:

> "Do you believe in God?" the lady inquired.
> "Sure, Mike!" he retorted briskly.

There is something dreadfully eloquent about this innocent short-circuit in communication.

One other very important remark is made by the author. The Yahi found strength in the incontrovertible fact that they were in the right. *"Of very great importance to their psychic health was the circumstance that their suffering and curtailments arose from wrongs done to them by others.* They were not guilt ridden."

Contrast this with the spectacle of our own country with its incomparable technological power, its unequalled material strength, and its psychic turmoil, its moral confusion and its profound heritage of guilt which neither the righteous declarations of Cardinals nor the moral indifference of "realists" can do anything to change! Every bomb we drop on a defenseless Asian village, every Asian child we disfigure or destroy with fire, only adds to the moral strength of those we wish to destroy for our own profit. It does not make the Viet Cong cause just; but by an accumulation of injustice done against innocent people we drive them into the arms of our enemies and make our own ideals look like the most pitiful sham.

Gradually the last members of the Yahi tribe died out. The situation of the survivors became more and more desperate. They could not continue to keep up their perfect invisibility: they had to steal food. Finally the hidden camp where Ishi lived with his sister and sick mother was discovered by surveyors who callously walked off with the few objects they found as souvenirs. The mother and sister died and finally on August 29, 1911, Ishi surrendered to the white race, expecting to be destroyed.

Actually, the news of this "last wild Indian" reached the anthropology department at Berkeley and a professor quickly took charge of things. He came and got the "wild man" out of jail. Ishi spent the rest of his life in San Francisco, patiently teaching his hitherto completely unknown (and quite sophisticated) language to experts like [Edward] Sapir. Curiously enough, Ishi lived in an anthropological museum where he earned his living as a kind of caretaker and also functioned, on occasion, as a live exhibit. He was well treated, and in fact the affection and charm of his relations with his white friends are not the least moving part of his story. He adapted to life in the city without too much trouble and returned once, with his friends, to live several months in his old territory, under his natural conditions, showing them how the Yahi had carried out the fantastic operation of their invisible survival. But he finally succumbed to one of the diseases of civilization. He died of tuberculosis in 1916, after four and a half years among white men.

For the reflective reader who is—as everyone must be today—deeply concerned about man and his fate, this is a moving and significant book, one of those unusually suggestive works that *must* be read, and perhaps more than once. It is a book to think deeply about and to take notes on, not only because of its extraordinary factual interest but because of its special quality as a kind of parable.

One cannot help thinking today of the Viet Nam war in terms of the Indian wars of a hundred years ago. Here again, one meets the same myths and misunderstandings, the same obsession with "completely wiping out" an enemy regarded as diabolical. The language of the Vigilantes had overtones of puritanism in it. The backwoods had to be "completely cleaned out," or "purified" of Indians—as if they were vermin. I have read accounts of American GI's taking the same attitude toward the Viet Cong. The jungles are thought to be "infested" with communists, and hence one goes after them as one would go after ants in the kitchen back home. And in this process of "cleaning up" (the language of "cleansing" appeases and pacifies the conscience), one becomes without realizing it a murderer of women and children. But this is an unfortunate accident, what the moralists call "double effect." Something that is just too bad, but which must be accepted in view of something more important that has to be done. And so there is more and more killing of civilians and less and less of the "something more important" which is what we are trying to achieve. In the end, it is the civilians that are killed in the ordinary course of events, and combatants only get killed by accident. No one worries any more about double effect. War is waged against the innocent to "break enemy morale."

What is most significant is that Viet Nam seems to have become an extension of our old western frontier, complete with enemies of another "inferior" race. This is a real "new frontier" that enables us to continue the cowboys-and-indians game which seems to be part and parcel of our national identity. What a pity that so many innocent people have to pay with their lives for our obsessive fantasies.

One last thing. Ishi never told anyone his real name. The California Indians apparently never uttered their own names, and were very careful about how they spoke the names of others. Ishi would never refer to the dead by name either. "He never revealed his own private Yahi name," says the author. "It was as though it had been consumed in the funeral pyre of the last of his loved ones."

In the end, no one ever found out a single name of the vanished community. Not even Ishi's. For Ishi simply means MAN.

How to Say Goodbye

Hullo; nice day; too cole; too hot; too much water-tee;
too much lazy-auna-tee; him lazy boy, smart boy; him
crazy-auna-tee; hims good; hims no good; bad man;
sleep; eat; work; sing; dance; I go; you go; you likey
him?; lice (rice), pishy (fish); bean-us; honey; labit
(rabbit); big one; little one; led (red); white; black;
hat-na (hat); shoes; camisa (Spanish for shirt); mahale
(Spanish for woman); lopa (rope); lopa pikta (rope
picture or moving pictures); candy-tee; soda wata;
whiskey-tee; smoke; doctor; big cheap (big chief);
dog; kitty-tee; coyote; chicken-a-tee; egg; apple;
owanga-tee; lemon; barnarna-tee; cracker; soap;
powder; medicine; chair; sit down; talk; how much
money-tee?; money; shoot; cut em; die man (death);
sick man; ole man; lady; mama; papa; sister; papoose
(baby); too much I smoke (fog); I all a time smoke;
put em away; you go get em; what's a matter-tee?; you
go pretty soon; long time; automobile; horse;
telephone; fire; pistol (gun); pike (fight); evelybody
happy; him cry; too much pina (pain); sheep-na; paka
(vaca, cow); tea; koppy (coffee); milik (milk); nipe
(knife); axa (axe); hatch (hatchet); papello (paper);
light; all a same.

This found poem is "an approximate" of Ishi's Eng-
lish vocabulary, compiled by Saxon T. Pope, Ishi's
physician and archery partner; from "Characteristics
of Ishi," in *Ishi the Last Yahi: A Documentary History*.

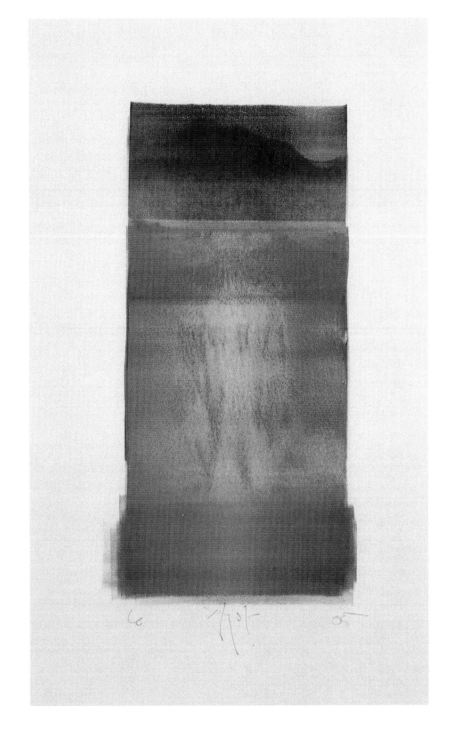

Selected Bibliography

Ishi in Two Worlds, by Theodora Kroeber. University of California Press, Berkeley, 1961.

> In addition to being Ishi's biography, *Ishi in Two Worlds* is one of the earliest books to tell the story of the genocide of California Indians. Recent anthropological research casts doubt upon some of the book's assumed facts about Ishi—for example, whether Ishi was in fact fully ethnically and culturally Yahi. Though it may not be able to be taken as the "Ishi Bible" as it was for many years, it remains a poignant recounting of Ishi's life and an important introduction to Ishi as an individual and as a craftsman, to the terms and issues of his life, and to the history of Native California as a whole.

Ishi, the Last Yahi: A Documentary History, by Robert F. Heizer and Theodora Kroeber. University of California Press, Berkeley, 1979.

> *Ishi, the Last Yahi* gathers a large selection of newspaper articles and academic papers on Ishi, as well as public documents and personal reminiscences on the conflict between Whites and the Yahi Indians that led to the latter's extinction. This book fills in many factual details that are not included in Theodora Kroeber's biography of Ishi.

Ishi in Three Centuries, edited by Karl Kroeber and Clifton Kroeber. University of Nebraska, Lincoln and London, 2003.

> *Ishi in Three Centuries* compiles a vast range of recent scholarship and essays into "the first substantial reexamination of the Ishi drama to be published in 40 years" (LA Times). In addition to archaelogocial studies that draw back the veils on some of the enduring questions about Ishi, the sons of anthropologist Alfred Kroeber offer penetrating and balanced commentary on the social and cultural relationships and dynamics surrounding Ishi.
>
> Karl Kroeber's essay "The Humanity of Ishi," included in *Ishi in Three Centuries*, is a particularly salient and moving exposition on the relationship between American Indian and White cultures, and the issue of appropriation or exploitation.

Ishi's Brain, Orin Starn. W. W. Norton & Co., 2005.
This is the story of anthropologist Orin Starn's sleuth-trail to the correspondence that revealed Ishi's brain had been held by the Smithsonian for decades, and that it had been donated to that institution by Alfred Kroeber. The book is narrated in memoir fashion, and tells of Starn's involvement with the people that ultimately revealed the location of Ishi's brain, as well as recounting the controversial process of repatriating Ishi's remains.

Wild Men: Ishi and Kroeber in the Wilderness of Modern America, by Douglas Cazaux Sackman. Oxford University Press, 2010.
A book about the relationship between Alfred Kroeber and Ishi.

A more extensive bibliography "intended to assist nonspecialists to pursue matters related to Ishi" may be found in *Ishi in Three Centuries*.

The works collected in *Songs from a Yahi Bow* appeared in the following books by their respective authors:

Ishi Means Man, Thomas Merton, Unicorn Press, 1968, 1976.
(This book contains a number of essays by Thomas Merton on Native American history in the United States and Mexico.)

Thieves of Paradise, Yusef Komunyakaa, Wesleyan University Press, 1998.

When the Tiger Weeps, Mike O'Connor, Pleasure Boat Studio: A Literary Press, 2004 ("Song of Ishi" was first published in *Dalmoma* magazine in 1976).

Additional poems about Ishi:

"The Concealment: Ishi the Last Wild Indian" by William Stafford.

"Ishi" by Louis Simpson.

Ishi Country: The Shadows and the Light by Gabriele S. Brown.

About the Authors

Scott Ezell

Scott Ezell's book-length poem *Petroglyph Americana* was published by Empty Bowl Press in 2010.

Yusef Komunyakaa

Yusef Komunyakaa won the Pulitzer Prize for Poetry in 1994 for *Neon Vernacular*.

Thomas Merton

Thomas Merton wrote more than 70 books on spirituality, social justice, and pacifism. He was a Trappist monk, and pioneered dialogue with prominent Asian spiritual figures, including the Dalai Lama, D.T. Suzuki, and Thich Nhat Hanh.

Mike O'Connor

Mike O'Connor is a poet, writer, and translator of Chinese. He has published eight books, most recently *When the Tiger Weeps* and *Unnecessary Talking: The Montesano Stories*. He has received an NEA Literature Fellowship and an Artist Trust Fellowship.

Jeff Hengst

Jeff Hengst is a painter and sculptor based in Seattle.

Editor's Acknowledgements

Thanks to Anne McCormick of the Merton Legacy Trust for permission to reprint "Ishi: A Meditation;" to Wesleyan Press for permission to publish "Quatrains for Ishi;" to Stephanie Dennis and Ellen Cernusak for sharing Gabriele S. Brown's *Ishi Country*; to Jeff Hengst for his paintings and friendship, and to Roland Crane of EM Fine Art for permission to publish Jeff's paintings; to Alicja Egbert of the Phoebe A. Hearst Museum of Anthropology for helping to arrange permission to publish Ishi's photo; to Richard Burrill for his correspondence and work on Ishi; to Douglas Newton and Mike Morical for editorial feedback; to Te Toh Titus for careful proof-reading; to Jason Schneiderman for his excellent design work; to Eran Haimberg for photographing "Two Worlds;" to Paul Sorrentino for an anthropological perspective on the text; to Gary Snyder for thoughts and suggestions during the work on this collection.

Thanks to publisher Jack Estes for his support of this book long before it resembled anything approximating a publishable manuscript.

I would like to express my gratitude to the late Karl Kroeber for his extremely cogent thoughts on Ishi, particularly Ishi's relationship to European-American society, contained in his essay "The Humanity of Ishi" and elsewhere.

About the Press

The press is named for "Pleasure Boat Studio," an essay written by Ouyang Xiu, Song Dynasty poet, essayist, and scholar, on the twelfth day of the twelfth month in the renwu year (January 25, 1043):

> "I have heard of men of antiquity who fled from the world to distant rivers and lakes and refused to their dying day to return. They must have found some source of pleasure there. If one is not anxious for profit, even at the risk of danger, or is not convicted of a crime and forced to embark; rather, if one has a favorable breeze and gentle seas and is able to rest comfortably on a pillow and mat, sailing several hundred miles in a single day, then is boat travel not enjoyable? Of course, I have no time for such diversions. But since 'pleasure boat' is the designation of boats used for such pastimes, I have now adopted it as the name of my studio. Is there anything wrong with that?"